Names We've Never Known

Karla K. Morton

Texas Review Press
Huntsville, Texas

FIRST EDITION, 2010
Requests for permission to reproduce material from this work should
be sent to:

Permissions
Texas Review Press
English Department
Sam Houston State University
Huntsville, TX 77341-2146

Acknowledgements

The author wishes to thank the following sources, where many
of the poems in this volume initially appeared:

descant
Langdon Review of the Arts
Borderlands
Southwestern American Literature
Becoming Superman
REAL: Regarding Arts and Letters
WFLAR (Wichita Falls Literary and Arts Review)
diversity Anthology
The Texas Review
Ardent
New Texas: A Journal of Literature and Culture

Library of Congress Cataloging-in-Publication Data

Morton, Karla K.
  Names we've never known / Karla K. Morton. -- 1st ed.
     p. cm.
  ISBN-13: 978-1-933896-39-7 (pbk. : alk. paper)
  ISBN-10: 1-933896-39-6 (pbk. : alk. paper)
  I. Title.
  PS3613.O77864N36 2010
  811'.6--dc22
                          2010005971

To the Man I Love

Contents

Names We've Never Known

Spring

"In the spring, we often stood beside a lilac bush . . .embracing for ten minutes at a time." —Charlton Heston, about his wife, Lydia

First comes the phlox, in a glorious schmear of purple butter
across wide lawns, in bar ditches; along lower hides of
    back pastures;
soon coral quinces; poxes of daffodils; all things
    bulbous-greenous will follow . . .
but the purple comes first

Across wide lawns and wider plains, we drive to Alpine;
    stop for a better view;
I step back into you like two stuck pages in a book.
Ponies kick up their heels at the first purple clouds of spring,
spryed by mere possibilities of rain

I step back into you; two stuck pages in an old linen book.
Wrap your arms around me now, for even rain we cannot
    know;
spry ponies buck at over-stuffed, piñata clouds;
hooves in schmears of purple

Wrapped together, we stand on these plains, between a
    beginning and an end,
but we can only know this moment; only know what
    came first;
pony hooves bridge the earth to the sky; buck at bolts of
    taffy lightning;
scatter bouquets of purple phlox at our feet.

Charmer

There was nothing he couldn't charm.
Standing on the edge of that irrigated
pond, they'd come for him, with three
taps on a Folgers can—water boiling

in anxious catfish. Cattle all but
skipped his way, rubbing up against
him; throwing back their heads, for a
scratch, like 800 pound kittens.

Everything and everyone succumbed
to his charms, except Grandma—I
just couldn't figure out their attraction . . .
Reported to have *never* had a sense

of humour, she seemed impervious
to his devious smile; his rogue ways,
bouncing off her stoic face
like a ping-pong ball to paddle;

her flared, lupin eyes, unyielding;
flinting; ready for combustion.
But one summer, after three weeks
of constant rain, I sank, wellie-deep,

in the milkdud clay, and she came,
pulling me out of my boots and
onto her—both of us falling back
in the mud; her laugh, softening

her face like the honeymoon
picture above their bed; her
cheeks; her eyes; bursting
into mounds of bluebonnets.

Decline of Nobility

Standing in the dog park, I watch the theory
of resemblance in
hounds and their people: the Catahoula's man,
rolling up his sleeves

to odd patches of tattoos; my lovely friend
and her sweet fuzzy
ball; the heavy-hipped St. Bernards and their hunched
grandpas; when up romps

Pontus, my squirrely-haired Scottish-Deerhound, dark
brown rabbit hanging
out of his mouth; haphazard ears jutting up.
Others chuckle. They've

seen me, dropping off my daughter to high school,
pajama bottoms
peeking below my coat; knowing my sink brims
in dirty dishes;

my dining room table's strewn with books, papers,
dictionaries; know
I'm unaffected by homeowner meetings;
PTA guilt; that

I dream of 13 acres on the Bosque;
custom boots; road trips
to San Angelo; that I'd gladly trade days
out with the girls, for

one perfect stanza . . . The greatest of hunters,
Deerhounds once sprawled on
castle floors while poets dined at the King's side;
entertaining his

royal court afterwards. It was even said
that those condemned to
death could buy their freedom with just three Deerhounds . . .
But these days, people

remain unimpressed, though I brag how he fetched
the morning paper,
then curled at my feet . . . while all day long, I poured
out my soul; making

sweet love with pen and paper and computer.

Passing Through Girdle Gulch

There is something in its snug
firmness; its resemblance of
a waist—the way it blossoms out around
two perfectly

shaped hills, like hips, and drops low;
that makes a cowboy stretch up
in his saddle, to get a better view;
that makes him pause

for a swig from his canteen;
and light up a smoke; and think
of the gentleness in hidden creek beds;
and where a man

might lay himself down to sleep . . .

Athiests

All those people who call themselves athiests,
should come on down to
Palo Duro Canyon . . . Let them walk that thin
trail between rattler

and cactus; let them watch thick canyon walls slide
from brown, to amber,
to dusty purple; let them stand beneath a
simple, geode night

sky, watching it crack open to a drusy
of stars . . . and *then* let
them ponder the possibility that there
just might be *something*—

some vast, wondrous Being, greater than themselves.

What Goes Unseen

"Vocatvus atque non vocatvus Deus a derit"
—*"Bidden or not bidden, God is present"*
—Carl Jung

The moon broods over her work,
arms crossed; her back to the night;
oblivious to circling planets;
waxing; waning;

braiding silks of corn; singing
songs of bloom to white, timid
blossoms; pulling up warm, chenille seas to
the chins of cold

shores...The sun pirouettes through
crescent windows; labouring;
dusting curved walls; streaking your hair—your head,
bent down over

open books, unfinished chores..
Always, *always*, there is work
waiting to be done . . . yet . . . Venus circles;
melons ripen;

moonflowers wait for the night.

Snakes

Mom taught me better than this . . .
yet, half an hour spent kissing
your lips, and I'm careless and dazed, easy
prey for fast strikes

from dark corners and back seats.
Later, I'll think of you, as
I reach down into the woodpile, gloveless;
my heart, exposed;

defenseless in open hands.

Squash Blossom

He was an
artist; a Native
American. Burned by long
hours in the New Mexico sun—
sitting on

the roadside,
selling his stone wares.
He was a small appliance
salesman, driving back home to Pampa.
It was his

wife's birthday.
Both hungry, proud men;
an old, cultural exchange.
Both coming home to smiling women—
one with the

beauty of
the new world in her
adobe; the other, with
the beauty of the old world, around
her pale neck.

Texas Kind of Tender

He was a Texas kind of tender—
though you'd never know it
unless you knew *him*; knew *Texas* . . .
Folks thought him mean—

he never pet the cattle he raised;
named them the appliance
he'd soon sell them for:
Microwave, IceBox, Deep Freeze . . .

Men, at his home, had to
step outside when they needed to go—
to save a nickel . . .
Cats, tossed out on roadsides

in pillowcased bundles,
were spared from starvation
and broken backs
by a single bullet to each head . . .

But things started to change that summer.
He went out, late at night,
and stepped on a rattler—
it bit him three times.

After that, the cats were saved
and the nickels spent . . .
That's when I showed up,
brought home like a stray

by his grandson,
loving him instantly—
my old witching blood
sensing a cool, deep
river of gentleness

far beneath a layer
of gruff so cracked,
you could turn an ankle in it...

He only hurt me once,
when he turned that well-worn shotgun
on his own failing body—
his last tender gesture

to spare a girl
who would have taken him in
and nursed him, spoon by spoon,
to his last, dying breath.

Summer at Texoma

—for the Cathros

The clouds call my name; the wind
rolls through my hair
Cicadas sing to my soul as if my body
wasn't there.

The lake ripples with life. She's cool
as iced gin.
She opens up wide and lets one more life in.

Summer at Texoma.
True-hearted friends.
Words and wine flowing.
Life, lived well,
never ends.

Functional Art

We would stop there, along the highway, every
season; those divine
stalks, shading the morning sun. A cardboard sign
told two prices—one

for his back, the other, for yours. But Dad seemed
hurried, and never
had time for us to gather our own, though my
hands ached to feel those

green lines and curling long leaves. "They're *beautiful!*"
I said to the man.
He hooked his thumbs in his overalls; looked up
at his field, "Yes. Yes

they are." I felt the lump in *his* throat; my eyes
swelled with *his* tears. I
read his face—feeling it in my every bone.
For weeks, we ate like

kings; warm butter sweetening each bite; just a
few shakes of salt; cobb
holders rusting from so much washing. And when
we'd had our fill, Mom

would can one more bushel in big quart jars; red
flecks of pimento
for her artist's eye. Six months later, ice storms
kept us a week from

school. I'd sneak in the pantry; squeeze myself in
the corner; and stare
at the wall—row after row of perfect line;
perfect symmetry—

tiny bits of yellow, like clear, morning sun.

Sign Language

—for Ed Patton

His was a generation
that nearly outlasted the
next—burying
all but two of his seven girls before
he turned 90.

Years before, with no hopes of
an heir for his fields, he sold
that Chico farm,
took up wildcatting; the untimely swing
of chain against

spinning steel, dropping fingers,
one by one, into oil black
holes—a part of
him buried first, like it should be—one for
every daughter.

Shaking Off the Shadow

> *— after reading that Larry Thomas, the 2008 Texas Poet Laureate, had worked at a prison for so many years . . .*

It was a profession that would scar
the most callous of men.
Punishment and tough-love and survival,
all sawed-off thick and smooth and hard
at the end of a billy club . . .
A hallowed ring lingering on steel bars;
a tight slap to the palm;
a warning thump into cement walls . . .

But when he came home,
he would cast aside that club,
and take off that prison uniform—
damp with harsh sweat and vicious looks;
and step into the shower,
turning his face up into the warmth;
feeling that dark haze of humanity
slip away,
like a big man's shadow
that stood,
blocking the daffodils
from the sun.

The Sacred

— Ekphrastic response to Jo Williams painting,
titled "Dream"

Fog seeps down, turning all things magic; sacred;
touching every stem,
every stone, every bent-headed cow. See how
she sleeps; her skin, in

colours of wintered grass; ripened wheat; fallen
leaves . . . You could lie down
behind her, arm warm across her creviced waist;
palm, stretched between hip

and rounded hip. God lingers there—inside each
sleeping woman's womb;
pipe dangling from His lips; reminiscing;
counting every soul;

curls of smoke hovering; descending like fog.

Not So Still Life

— Ekphrastic response poem to Jo Williams painting,
titled "Among the Cattails"

January ice
laces the slow river like
delicate

milk-glass; and below,
cold trout zig-zag from rock to
rock to stem,

dreaming of fattened,
summer mayflies . . . Above them,
cattails, tall

and reedy—their brown
suede caps beginning to burst—
pale, silky

seeds floating like bugs;
drooling fish lips wait—knocking
on wet glass.

Corpus Christi Man

There was something about him
that reminded her of the beach.
Corpus Christi, Key West, Carmel . . .
in him it was all the same—
the salt, the turbulence,
the abundance of life
teeming just under the surface.

She could picture him there
on the coast,
a white, collarless shirt
barely buttoned;
khaki pants rolled up to his knees;
the waves reaching out for him
again and again
like her arms ached to do.

And when she finally
held him close
and saw the flicker of lightning
in his eyes,
and heard the thunder
welling up from the back of his throat,
she realized
this is how it felt
to hold the wind—
to feel the passion and power
of an unleashed midnight storm.

Directionally Impaired

She always wanted
to live in the mountains
or on the coast.
It was *there*
she felt most at home;
there
where she understood
the theory of a compass—
knowing NORTH
would always be
to the right of WEST;
knowing no matter
which direction
she traveled,
sunset would always
lead her back home.

Texas Heirlooms

They called her "Legs" back then—
back in her late 40's; her early 50's...
back when she worked at Bell Helicopter,
and had to walk clear across Plant 5
to get to her office . . .
I recall her fluster in dressing—
her detail; her *fuss*
over the perfect skirt hemline—
how it had to fall *just* to the curve of her calves . . .

And I can see her, as I look at my daughter—
something about the shape of the eyes; the line of the
    lip . . .
but further down . . .
Bluejeans. She *only* wears bluejeans—
fanatic over just the right style; the right cling;
the right length; the perfect back-pocket placement . . .
inherently knowing how they enhance those tall, slim
    limbs . . .

You told me today, you loved my legs,
as you traced two generations
of long bone and shaped muscle
with your fingertips —
the look of sheer, male pleasure
following in your eyes . . .
and I understood, in an instant,
fashion's impact on society;
understood why Mother
never wasted her money
on fine china and sterling sugar tongs . . .

What Really Makes the Stars Shine

He's learning me well.
Plotting my freckles and moles
like Galileo.
The stars glare down, jealous of
my hot skin; his cool fingers

What Calls from the Dark

Into obvious danger, the frog leapt,
saved only by the dog's momentary
curiousity. I swept it up in my hands
and it sat, without struggle, without fear.

It began croaking as I held it, a low
rumble, vibrating inside its dark body,
like the oncoming thunder, quivering
the windows; the roof; the walls.

My animals cowered to the sound—beasts,
afraid of nothing, sought shelter; acquiescing
to a power beyond their earthly senses . . .
But I had a dog once, who barked at

storms—barked until he drove himself
mad. The rainiest season on record, he
paced trenches along the fence line—
back and forth; back and forth.

Even indoors, he couldn't be soothed—
sensing dark clouds, yelping in circles—
delirious, crazed; unable to find the source
of the sounds . . . There's a man, downtown,

his whole world in a wire cart; says he hears
things, voices sometimes—archaic and bent . . .
People walk by, holding tight to childrens' hands;
unwilling to hear what calls him from the dark.

Standing by the Bok Choy
Central Market, Plano Texas

They seemed to grow greener
the longer I stood there, watching them—
the bok choy, the celery root,
the green cabbage, the artichokes . . .
sweetening, ripening, becoming fuller
under the warm touch and rolling accent
of those they had grown up with—
the sounds and the feel
of the fields and the sun and the plow,
wrapped in the brown hands,
and the musical mezcla tongue . . .

The earth and onions know no borders.

They were smiling—
expertly nurtured and picked and cut and stacked.
And I felt unworthy . . .
unworthy to claim such treasures as my own—
as if a nanny had raised my children;
as if I had no right at the dinner party
to say *thank you*,
when someone commented
on my perfectly *flawless* avocados . . .

A Rare Man

It took a rare man with an old soul,
to see her beauty;
a man who's heart
wandered out in the wilds—
beyond the harsh, artificial glare of city lights—
where the true colour of midnight
could still be seen . . .
and recognized it
in her eyes . . .

A man who held the old ways
in the blood of his veins;
who could feel eternity
transcending her Romanesque curves . . .

A man who communed with the Earth;
a man who, like the crickets,
could still hear the sweet song
that swept between her bare thighs
when she walked . . .

What Makes a Thing Strong

Mother told me
I was a child of the wind,
brought into this world
in a September bluster—
eyes closed, back arched,
mouth open and screaming...
a powerful force indeed.

And as far back as I can remember,
I've prefered the full, twirly skirts
and long hair
and ruanas tossed over my shoulders—
anything that can fly in the breeze.
Always hoping for a strong wind—
for the perfect Diva exit.

But I've learned it's all about restraint,
of patiently *catching* the wind . . .
Sure, there will be times
when we need the heavy lifting—
the draft in the road,
the tailwind, the blue northern,
the all-out tornado . . .

But power, *true power*,
comes by controlling your strength . . .
Pianissimo is much more difficult than forte.
What tamed control it takes to stir bells one and three,
instead of the whole windchime.
What delicate grace there is in the slow furl of a flag . . .

There is no strength greater than the gentlest touch;
no power as mighty
as the tender brush of wayward hairs from your eyes.

Amarillo Embers

Traveling at night, just north of Claude,
I topped a small hill to find the lights of Amarillo
burning amber on the horizon—
as though She were a great campfire
that had wound down to hot embers—
Her cowboy lying close by in the dark—
his hat across his sleeping face;
bedded up against the January cold . . .

And She was restless, laying there beside him,
whispering,
"Roll over, Cowboy. Come closer . . ."
knowing all it would take
is the stir of his breath,
and the lightest touch
of a dry root, or a fallen feather,
or the slightest feel of his hair,
to burst Her anxious embers
back into flame . . .

Austin Embrace

She welcomes with a rush of light;
with busy, wide roads, and old tiny green niches;

a home for those needing a place to belong;
a sanctuary for the lost; a mecca for the hungry;

a place where old Texas courts the new;
where art and business shine the same boots;

the place where the cowboy
converges with the rest of the world.

A soapdish of politics and eccentrics and academics,
in an aging limestone lavabo . . .

And yet, for all she gives, all she ever asks in return
is that you remember her when you go,

and that you leave the kitchen light on
for the wanderer following behind . . .

A Life of Luck and Ladies

An old sea captain once told me
it's bad luck to change a boat's name;
said he'd never take the chance—
would never put a crew at risk
by angering the sea gods
in a re-named ship;
said you should just leave all those women
well enough alone.

I saw so many of those old ladies
along the intracoastal,
broken down and rusted
from time and salt and age:
Suzy Q, Ms. Simon, Barbara Jean,
Miss Evelyn, Sara Ann . . .

How they must have shined in their prime,
back when their buxom namesakes
stood on the docks,
and wrapped luck
around their lovers' neck,
and passionately kissed them off to sea . . .

And I thought of their men—
all those men who loved them.
Men who needed no photo or wedding band;
men who carried
their hearts on their hulls;
men who trusted their lives
to the fickle whims of the sea.

Cantaloupe Song

With the patience of time,
they burst from their seeds
in a growing, slow-motion dance.
With many arms, like Kuan Yin,
curling in graceful Hawaiian sway—
stretching stronger and longer
each moment of each day—
the song of the cantaloupe plants.

The living hear nothing
but just the sigh of the Wind,
but still we search for this sound . . .
when all we have to do is
fall to our knees,
and lay our ears upon the ground.

Close your eyes, listen closely,
beyond the heartbeat of the Earth.
there . . . *feel* it growing strong . . .
That is the music
that curls the vines and and courts the bees,
that brings fruit to our mouths
and mankind to his knees.
That is the cantaloupe song.

We should plant them around
the quiet headstones of death,
and let them grow full and wild—
their song, soothing the spirits
of those we have lost,
like a soft lullaby to a child.

Sing to our angels, wherever they are,
for you fill us with such great hope—
that they will think of us with each sweet serenade,
as we do them . . . with each taste of cantaloupe.

Lost Beyond the Rush

I found this empty file in my computer.
I suppose I had created it
in a moment of intense inspiration,
but got caught up in the daily repetitions of life
and forgot it . . . never quite getting it back.

How is it those moments
can come and go?
That the dream we had awoken to
vanishes in a blink?
We remember . . .
no . . . can't even tell you
what it was we remember about it,
just the feeling—yes, a good feeling—
something about
a sea cave's entrance
with wild waves splashing all around
but it's gone so quickly,
lost in the time it took
to brush your teeth
and wash your face . . .
sometimes glimpses return a little later,
but usually, they're gone forever.

I remember now
standing here,
wiping the toothpaste and water
from my mouth and hands.
I remember a glimpse of *our* dream—
holding hands as the priest tied his scarf around them . . .
And I find myself wishing
he had tied the knot a little tighter,
and that all those good moments
hadn't come and gone so quickly
like water rushing over our hands.

Superconductivity

When the two men met,
she felt her worlds collide . . .

And when they extended their arms
in manly greeting,
she watched,

wondering if their hands
would be thrown apart—
repelled like the opposite ends of a magnet,

or if they would cling together
in a loop of perpetual electrical current
brought on by the rush of recognition—

both having been magnetized
by the steady slow strokes of her skin . . .

Purple Pathways

There's a reverence in purple
like no other colour...
of gold-sashed royalty,
and tightly wound turbans
framing flawless, dark African faces;
of draped crucifixes
inside hushed church walls;
of a corner building brimming
with old books,
marking the evolution of mankind...

It's the colour of magic,
and mountain fog;
of February births and wild irises;
the lingering stain of childhood
inside the rim of white baseball caps...

And it's the heart,
just after its final beating --
when the soul reaches up
to grasp it,
like a purple doorknob,
turning it ever so slightly
to the right...
pushing open a pathway
just wide enough
to let the soul slip through
to the other side.

Fearless

My brother, a former F-16 pilot,
said the trick to flying
is complete and total trust.
He said when you fly into thick clouds,
or heavy fog,
or the emptiness of night,
you have to *know*,
have an unfaltering faith
that your instruments are calibrated correctly,
that your gas tanked is filled,
that the steel of the body
is welded firm all around you . . .
And then believe it.
Otherwise, he said,
doubt alone can bring you down.

He had lost a friend years ago . . . a good friend
who was flying back from combat,
who had become disoriented in the dark.
Who, not believing his instruments,
had locked onto his own visual—the moon.
But it wasn't the moon,
it was the light of a train,
and within moments, he'd crashed head on
into the ground.

How easy it is *not* to trust.
To doubt the instrument panel
or the words we hear
or our own inner voice,
or the course of the moon,
or even the undeniable hand of Fate.

And when this happens,
when doubt overtakes us
and we have lost all faith,
we become afraid . . .
And it's in fear that we fall—
whether it be in the mind or the body or the heart . . .
the heart most of all.

Love *should* be about the flying, not the falling, I say
as I call to you, I come to you.
I come to know the thrill of the cloudy unknown,
and the dark of the night—
trusting you more than the measure of the moon,
believing in the steel of your arms.

Vegas From 30,000 Feet

It seemed so fitting
that the extremes of humanity
would live on the edge
of *nature's* extremes—
of harsh desert and unforgiving earth.
So fitting that the hedonism of man
be kept within the checks and balances
of drought, and death, and hidden scorpions.

Beating the Bushes

There was a place on her headboard
her hands immediately went . . .

comforting grooves in the iron
where her fingers instinctively fled

when he decided to take her in the night;
physically preparing herself for the pain of his touch—

his heavy grip on her breasts
which tightened with his body

as though he were riding a Harley—
changing, gear to gear,

accelerating, faster and faster
up a curvaceous mountain road.

But her eyes flew ahead of him,
like startled doves—

up to the ceiling,
then out the tall windows,

and into the night;
into the safety of the sky—

higher and higher
until the only thing she could think about

was how cool and dark the wind must feel
along the rim of Palo Duro . . .

Ultimate Sacrifice

There was nothing she wanted more in this life
than to have a child of her own . . .

She thought about that
as she laid there, on the table,
beaten—still covered in bruises;
the doctor working the DNC between her legs.

33 years later,
she still cried that same day, every June,
her body having crossed over
into early menopause.

her womb
having only been given one chance.

Growth Chart

She insinuated I was a bad mother—

I never tracked his birthdays
on the inside pantry doorframe;
I can't remember how long he measured,
or how much he weighed when he was born;
I can't remember the names of most of his teachers . . .

But what I don't tell her—

is how my thumb and forefinger
wrapped completely around his tiny thigh
when he was born;

or how, when he was four,
he was as tall as me when I squatted down, arms opened,
ready to catch his running embrace—
and how we would tumble over together, laughing . . .

or how, when he crawls into bed with me,
cursing his early morning classes,
to hug me good-bye,
and then drives off to school,
I cry sweet, mother tears . . .
my heart marking the moment
he became more man than boy.

An Ordinary Moment of Extraordinary Beauty on Northside Drive

The morning after
my family's fourth death
in four months,
I woke from a wonderfully
mundane dream—
a dream about
an ordinary morning;
of finding my children
sleeping in my bed;
of rising, completely rested,
and walking across
sun-warmed wooden floors
and raising the wintered windows
for the first gasp of spring...

And days later,
as the hammering grief
pummeled through the funeral dirge,
my mind drifted back
to something I had seen the day before . . .
to this *horse*
this untethered, *magnificent*
grey mare
running barebacked and wild
through the streets of Ft. Worth,
the musk of the Trinity
flaring her nostrils,
the green of freedom
delirious in her hooves.

Why I Write

It was that wood box she kept in her closet—
from some dark, secret
place. She'd pull it out, on occasion, two lids
fanning outward in

tiny maroon velvet shelves, full of treasures.
I'd touch each of them,
trying on rings and bracelets and necklaces,
and she'd bend down to

lift bits of paper and letters—to get them
out of my way . . . notes
she would open, one by one, and smile over,
and gently fold back

up . . . I soon realized *those* were the real treasures—
letters that would turn
her eyes to soft sapphires; and by the way one
hand crept to her neck,

pearls began growing in her throat with each word.

Alvarado Coy

He always knew he'd either be a Baptist
preacher or a ditch
digger. It wasn't until he had a few
years under his belt,

and a few Sunday sermons under his hat,
when he realized that
church was full of too damn many women. "All
things equal," he'd say,

"I prefer the company of the ditches."

First Lady Gowns

— TWU's display of Texas First Lady Gowns

Behind cleaned windows, they stand,
propped up by smiling manikins;
bits of royal DNA still caught in zippers;
tucked in tiny beading; embedded in

last minute alterations. Ears against
the glass, we hear them, in voices of
fabric rustle; clinking Waterford; the
humm of Mozart between sequins.

This is the line between the common
and the immortal; threads that hold their
transformation from years long gone;
nights as dreamy as lamp lit skin, when

they waltzed into history—bits of nerves
for that first ball dance; secret words
between husbands and wives . . . A turn; a twirl;
then one more night alone; one more night

before an eternity of eyes—hanging on the back
of the bathroom door; or strewn across the loveseat;
or crumpled on the floor of the Governor's Mansion,
beside that big, four-posted, mahogany bed.

Lightning Bolt Grins

Walking through this pumpkin patch,
I can't help but remember watching

my laughing toddlers,
running through the orange mazes,

stradling the biggest ones, and riding them,
like quarter-fed supermarket horses.

Or that cool, cloudy night,
when you pulled me down

between all those great, puffed heads,
my knees, damp with dark October grass—

holding on tight; rocking together
under a moon as hidden as the

unseen faces around us—clandestine,
triangle eyes, and lightning bolt grins.

Belly Dancing Sirens

Out of the country for a week, the longest
he'd *ever* been off
from work since he started, at 13. He fumed
to learn tornados

diverted airline traffic to Baton Rouge.
A punctual man,
he insisted he *had* to get back, despite
the pleas of his wife,

and the National Weather Center; renting
a car and driving
down to New Orleans, to find his car, submerged
where he parked it, with

no street above water to get back home. North,
we were led, in an
odd, bright night; across the only open, yet
deserted pathway—

a bridge. That's when we saw them—two on the left
side; one on the right;
gyrating their exposed, slender bellies; their
thin grey hips, in slow,

mesmerizing dances; arms up; open to
the sky, deadly tails
down deep in the Ponchartrain. Spellbound, we'd
stopped,
until I noticed

they were slyly creeping closer together—
around us. "GO!" I
shrieked, and he floored it, the wake of our rental,
drowned out by the whrrr
of silent laughter; the electricity
of a bell-less dance;
the only females that *ever* led him back
to bed; late for work.

When the Waters Rise Up

There are those of the desert
who still follow the old ways,
the old paths.

Like the builders
who only lay bricks and rock-work,
and foundations in the new moon.
It's *then*, they say,
when the waters rise up to the surface,
and the structures are less likely
to crack and weaken
when time and age
and the gravity of the full moon meet.

And there are the gardeners,
who only plant in this same new moon.
Who swear the waters come up through
the earth, to nourish the young seedlings.

I thought about these waters
as I followed the stream to the river.
It was the old and natural way—
the way of the deer and the bear
and the Natives before us.

Nature *knows* the pull of the moon;
blesses the path of the moving waters.

Come now, my love,
let us revel in these old ways.
Let us marry
in the dark new moon;
when all things hold firm;
when the waters rise up
to feed the roots beneath our feet.

West Texas Man

He's a West Texas man,
never bothering with the trivial;
with a faith as wide as the sky,
as deep as cool water running . . . running
miles beneath this broken hardscrabble—
where life and death are daily occurences.
Flowers are a luxury.

He's a West Texas man,
grown strong and lean,
his chest, barely giving, like a steer—
all horn and bone and sinew;
a man who wakes up believing . . . believing
he and his own will survive another day.
Cactus blooms yellow and pink.

He's a West Texas man,
where snakes and coyotes
still outnumber the people;
where hawks rest on fenceposts—the tallest perch for
          miles—
like silent Angels, watching . . . watching.
A man who wraps his love in words and bluebonnet
          seeds
and hangnail moons.

He's a West Texas man,
with no need for rosaries or cement saints,
knowing there's no greater faith than lightning rods on
the plains—
steel rain prayers, calling . . . calling . . .
reaching higher than the highest church steeples.
A man who wraps his woman in his arms each night;
her hair, the tender scent of rain-drenched wildflowers.

Crybaby

All day long, I'd keep up with my brother,
to prove I wasn't the crybaby he always
said I was. We'd string trot lines, sing
Paul Simon songs; eat up the ammunition

Grandpa gave us to shoot the moccasins.
20 acres of catfish farm, and real guns,
made for the perfect childhood . . .
But then came the dusk, when we'd haul in

our long-whiskered loot—the cold, slick muscle
of them, curling, whipping, bleeding our hands;
fighting for freedom. We'd carry them in 5 gallon
buckets back to the house—to the sentinel

metal chair and table by the garden hose.
It was my job to hold the light while he cut off
their squawking heads, and de-bone them . . .
But to this day, I've never learned to clean a fish—

turning my head at each chance of education;
trying to fight back those embarrassing tears—
that surging swell of tender; silently begging for
forgiveness with each wet rip of the knife.

Turkey Vultures

I saw him there
on the side of the road
nestled in the mexican blankets
and wine cups
and fading bluebonnets,
his sweet little coon face
quiet
and close-eyed
in the deepening, spring dusk.

And just beyond
in the shadows of the shade,
stood seven dark angels,
red-faced and somber,
patiently waiting
to take him on home.

Death of a Son

My love runs deep
in unseen rivers in the earth,
surrounded by moss so green,
it's black.

Apricot nuts lay,
tossed about the banks,
like scattered almonds;
rose roots hang down from above.

This is where you rest,
my child; my love.
Snake holes guide the moonlight down,
and cast it on the river,

in tiny shards
as thin as wine glass to the lips.
Come down to the water;
splash moonlight across your face;

sit down on the cool moss . . .
Let me think of you there, barefoot;
fishing pole in one hand;
half-eaten apricot, in the other;

head cocked in laughter;
knowing the face of God;
becoming one with the river;
the roses; the moon.

Wow

I donned blue and black flippers;
a yellow snorkel and mask; and
set out to see life from the fishes'
point of view; following their brainy

coral and gentle, swaying seaweed.
We swam along until we came upon
this huge drop-off by the reef;
where all we little fish gathered—

instinctively understanding
the turquoise was ours; the aqua
was ours; even the pale, clear, teal
was ours...but not this deep, endless

colbalt—a blue beyond our knowing;
a blue made for creatures greater
than ourselves; a great canyon's edge
that left us humbled; afraid to trespass.

We hovered, unable to go beyond;
all we could do was just look into this abyss,
and move our fishy lips over and over again,
mouthing one single, silent, exclamatory word . . .

Parting the Waters

He always talked about it,
about building the Hoover Dam in '32.
He talked about sleeping under the stars,
and parting the river,
and writing love letters to my grandmother
in the dim lamp light.
Her eyes were just so blue . . . he used to say,
I didn't have the nerve to ask her to marry me.

His favourite Dam story was that night in Black Canyon,
battling a porcupine in his tent—
needles like small, sharpened white bones
embedding all over him, traveling further inside his body
with each movement he made . . .

It was a sign, he'd insisted,
for just *one* of those needles
could have easily pierced his heart or his lungs . . .
but they didn't.
He took it as God's promise that he wouldn't die,
so he volunteered for the High Scalers—
that dare-devil group of men who first worked
the Dam, 500 ft. above the Colorado River,
drilling out the rock by hand—
fearless on the treacherous ledges;
the aborted quills tucked safely in his boot.

He sent some of them to my grandmother
in a betrothal letter --
I will come home to you, he wrote,
I will know the blue-deep of your eyes once again,
and we will marry.

How lucky are those who believe in signs—
mere mortals, sure-footed with confidence—
able to move the highest of mountains;
able to part
the mighty surge of the waters . . .

Rooster's Gotta Crow

They roamed the island like they owned it—
pecking and strutting and mating, with no regard

for our sensitive tourist dispositions—our love of
late-night drinking; our subsequent need to sleep

through dawn's obnoxiously early arrival—pulled in
by their great inhalation; the backward thrust of

decorated heads; their piercing attack
that would wake up God Himself, should He have

fallen asleep on His great throne; the worldly remote,
limp across His white-robed lap . . . And we'd go out,

trying to shush those thick-bodied birds, shaking
their mangrove perches, but they refused to be stilled;

refused to be quieted; as if they were ancient soldiers
called up for duty, despite our insults and curses;

instinctively defending mankind from the evil surge
of night; saving us from the darkness of ourselves.

Unlatched

He was a king among men—
having traveled the world,
and climbed Kilimanjaro;

his body, strong and lean;
his skin, tanned; his eyes,
rich and luminous with all

he had seen . . . But when he
found himself in Bangkok,
in front of the golden, draped

Buddha, he was humbled with
mortality; with a fleeting sense
of *self* . . . And he bought a wooden

cage full of finches; tucked
unspoken prayers in the tiny
folds of their wings; then set

them free—to rise beyond the
reach of earthbound man; up
into the great, open eyes of God.

When the Rest of Texas Sleeps

you rise in the quiet,
over my still body—
a black moon;
a sliver of bath light
caught in your wide pupils,
like tiny stars;

your touch, singing through me
before I fully wake—
a wordless tune,
breaking open the night
in arch of back,
and gasp of dark, sacred air . . .

House Hunting Criteria

It took a long long time
to find a house of my own . . .
I must have seen at least 40 houses,
but so many were just too young,
I couldn't identify with them.
The only story *their* foundation could boast
was 8 months of sawdust . . .

No . . . I was looking for something older,
something with a past—
something with memories
and ghosts and big trees.
Something with a history
of rats in the attic and overflowing toilets
and litters of wild kittens birthed under the porch.
A Jewish grandmother
whose wooden floors
ached and moaned under my feet,
whose 6th stair was as soft as my stomach,
a place who, *oy vey*,
kept me out of the sun.

I needed a place used to ice storms
and straight-line winds and teenage boys
and old dogs leaning up against it.
A place that stood because it wanted to,
not just because some man built it.
I needed a place that needed me
just as much as I needed her.

I have memorized the plumber's number.
I have witnessed the swarm of the termite.
I have eaten my way through funerals,
and passed out in bathtubs.

I have learned that scorpions travel in pairs,
and how to smother fires with salt.
I have endlessly borrowed powdered sugar
from my neighbours, and guilted my children into calling . . .
oh yes, *oy vey*,
give me an old house that shows her teeth when she smiles;
a house that's as lovely and peaceful and spoiled
and grumpy in the mornings
as me.

In Your Prime

That's how I'll always remember him—
a crewcut and white t-shirt,
short sleeves snug with muscle;
drawing in the fire of that cigarette,

then tossing it,
like a tiny, opaque bolt of white lightning;
and raising that post-hole digger
with two mighty arms,

and slamming it down, deep into the earth,
pulling up a rusted mouthful of ungiving red clay
over and over, until it reached that
perfect fence-pole depth.

All that fire feeding his strength;
arcing his abdomen . . .
the physical magnificence
of a man in his prime . . .

He gave up cigarettes years later,
growing old and frail,
succumbing to age;
no longer courting the flame

like you still do—
your hands, guiding it
into the tobacco;
that swell of heat

flaring through your drag.
Your body, your arms—
stallion lean and strong,
reaching for me now

while the fire flows
hot and strong through your body;
your unyielding lips
tasting like man; like smoke.

May Comes to Denton County

in a sprinkling of ponies;
horse ranches littered with tiny
sunning foals, their mares grazing
close by. Children, sensing the

end of school, bolt, like thirsty
herds to water, running crazed
into three hot months of flip-flops
and late bedtimes.

And on Saturday nights, girls
don eyeliner and short dresses;
long legs wobbling in mother's
heels, like eager, newborn colts.

The Old That's Worth Hanging On To

There's an incredible old oak tree
just around the corner—
huge trunk, deep roots,
two massive branches
coming out from the middle...
but that last blue norther'
ripped one of them off,
leaving the remaining branch
so off balanced,
so seemingly out of place.

The neighbours all told her
she should cut that thing down,
that it had become an eyesore
so obviously half of a whole.
But she just shook her head
as she looked across the sofa
to the empty blue rocking-recliner,
picturing the man
who used to occupy that seat,
the man who helped his father
plant that tree . . .

And further on, into downtown,
there's a white marble memorial
to the Civil War veterans—
complete with
two now-defunct water fountains
one originally meant
for black lips
the other, for white

and, oh, the civil rights activists
show up from time to time, fists flying,

their media crews in tow,
demanding it be brought down,
calling it an obvious display
of a society ripped in two,
an emotional eyesore

but the town just sits
and shakes its wise head,
knowing some of the old
should *always* be seen,
knowing some deep roots
are *still* alive and well,
knowing sometimes, *some things*
are too immense to be forgotten.

Ice Blue

It had been 28 years
since she last slept in that room.
The walls and drapes and furniture were different,
but it was still *her* room—
that place where she dreamed;
that same magical window that transported her eyes
up into the ever-changing sky,
where those hopes took shape.
She put her hand on the cold pane,
and felt a few still in there,
alive and lingering in the glass . . .

And she visited with her parents --
a good, long, unrushed visit,
not realizing before then
how absolutely beautiful her mother was—
her face, perfect with every curved line of time;
her eyes, having become a lighter, brighter blue with age . . .

Eyes that reminded her of this old oak tree
she had passed on the way—
big and round and wide;
standing strong in an open field;
Christmas lights wrapped *completely*
around its huge trunk up to its tiniest top twigs—
hundreds of lights that burned so bright, so white,
that they were barely blue . . .
the colour of December breath;
the colour of moonlight through the window;
the colour of her mother's eyes.

And she could only hope that one day,
she might age as gracefully—
simply growing more beautiful with each passing night;

the moon wrapping her,
again and again,
in pale lights of ice blue.

Love Letter

I thought about you tonight
as I was flying back in that little plane,
about how our skin would
brush together there,
in that tiny seat;
how you would lift
your arm around me,
and I would nestle into your shoulder,
and let my head fall back
as we watched the tops of the clouds
through that square, white window;

how our breath would hitch
as the plane suddenly emerged from them
again and again,
into the clear sunshine
and 10,000 foot drop-off
down to earth.

And as we were landing,
I thought about our lips,
and that moment right before we kiss—
the same feeling
as right before the wheels touched down;
when the plane was letting go
of the throttled power;
giving in to the vulnerable pull
of gravity.

Never Meant to Last

He was never a patient man.
His anger would burst like a canyon's flash flood . . .
but nothing greened in its wake,
no desert flowers bloomed
when the raging waters receded.

And there was this one afternoon
she couldn't find her keys
she rattled and laughed and carried on,
endlessly searching through her cavernous purse,
oblivious to the dark clouds forming,
to the storm about to explode.

And when he erupted,
he grabbed and dumped her purse on the hood of her car,
mocking its contents: rocks, twigs, a plastic toy soldier,
lip gloss, a mirror, three books of poems,
a feather, ocean glass,
notebooks pencils hankies wallet, ah . . . and then *finally*
 the keys.
He couldn't understand it—why she carried such junk,
how on earth could she consider these things *precious*
 treasures?

Twenty years later, he mellowed a bit.
Perhaps, he thought, his turbulent heart
had been broken all along;
and that quadruple by-pass had fixed it,
helping him to understand his daughter's nonsense a
 little better;
to understand why she loved such temporary things—
why she would choose a pearl wedding ring
instead of an everlasting heirloom diamond.

And he found himself hoping
his great-great-great-granddaughter
would cherish that empty silver ring one day,
its pearl having turned back to dust long ago,
finally understanding
that what makes something precious,
is the knowledge,
then the *realization*,
that *nothing* was ever meant to last.

Horseshoes

There is an elemental
sound in horseshoes—a firmness
when iron hits ground; of strength and foundation.
Double-backed on

your wide, brown mare, it was a
simple ceremony, my
fist full of pale Casablanca lilies
and moonflowers,

then you behind me, the warm
trust of horse beneath us, dressed
in her iron shoes. Generations later,
this is how they'll

remember us, in some old
photo of our reception,
me, barefoot in a puddle of white cloth
and cooling earth,

watching you—concentrating,
poised like Mercury taking
flight—flanges, like tiny wings, at the heels
of your worn boots;

and they'll know those unseen sounds
that follow—that timeless ring
of metal joining metal, then the earth;
those unflinching

arms, ready to catch what falls.

Anniversary

Every night after supper, you stroll these
drought-laden fields, pipe in one hand,

walking stick in the other; making love
to a land as cracked and pieced as thick,

broken glass; only to return smiling—to a
woman, barren for years . . . looking at me

like a crop of sweet corn—green and full
of ripe husks, like sons, too many to name.

Names We've Never Known

When old man Prunty died, he left them—
two dogs my children loved on every
vacation for at least 13 summers. I never
thought to ask him what he'd named them

so many years ago—it just didn't seem
to matter. To us they'd always be Fluffy
and Yappy—perfectly matched by any
Native American standard. Two people

in town took over their care, but I
couldn't help but notice how happy they
seemed to see us this year—to see my
kids, all grown up; still stopping by

the fence, arms now long enough to reach
over the chain link, instead of elbow deep
through the bottom holes; cooing sweetness;
rubbing their up-stretched chins . . . I wonder

what they secretly call *us*; or what they
called old man Prunty. I wonder if they
even know he's long gone from this
world—still giving a quick thump of tail

and raising hopeful heads, ears forward,
each time that back door opens; still
waiting to hear his soft voice calling
those names we've never known.